The King Cake Baby

The King Cake Baby

By Keila V. Dawson
Illustrated by
Vernon Smith

PELICAN PUBLISHING COMPANY

To all my New Orleans and Louisiana family and friends, who understand, appreciate, and strive to preserve our unique culture — K.V.D.

For my daughter, Amelia, to whom everything I do is dedicated — V.S.

The word "Pelican" and the depiction of a pelican are trademarks of Pelican Publishing Company, Inc., and are registered in the U.S. Patent and Trademark Office.

Library of Congress Cataloging-in-Publication Data

Dawson, Keila V., author.
 The King Cake Baby / by Keila V. Dawson ; illustrated by Vernon Smith.
  pages cm
  Summary: In this New Orleans version of The Gingerbread Man, the King Cake Baby, a small figure that is traditionally baked inside a king cake during Carnival season, escapes and encounters various local characters as he runs across the French Quarter, heading for the Mississippi River. Includes a recipe for king cake.
  ISBN 978-1-4556-2013-5 (pbk : alk. paper) -- ISBN 978-1-4556-2014-2 (e-book) 1. Gingerbread boy--Adaptations--Juvenile fiction. 2. Carnival--Juvenile fiction. 3. King cakes--Juvenile fiction. 4. New Orleans (La.)--Juvenile fiction. [1. Mardi Gras--Fiction. 2. King cakes--Fiction. 3. New Orleans (La.)--Fiction.] I. Smith, Vernon, 1974- illustrator. II. Title.
 PZ7.1.D39Ki 2015
 [E]--dc23
                          2014028532

Printed in China
Published by Pelican Publishing Company, Inc.
1000 Burmaster Street, Gretna, Louisiana 70053

The King Cake Baby

Once upon a time, an old Creole woman
and an old Creole man lived in New Orleans.

They wanted to celebrate Kings' Day on January 6,
so the woman decided to make a king cake.

First, she mixed the sugar, salt, butter, eggs, yeast, milk, and flour to make the dough.

Then she made a cinnamon-sugar
filling and a cream-cheese icing.

The old woman carefully formed the dough into an oval shape and placed the cake into the oven to bake.

Lastly, she made purple, green, and
gold sugar sprinkles for the topping.

The old woman went to the kitchen drawer to get the king cake baby that belonged inside the cake. But when she opened the drawer, the baby jumped out and ran away!

She chased the plastic baby, shouting, "Stop! Stop! You belong in the king cake!" But the King Cake Baby ran on and teased:

The baby ran out the door, over the porch, and past the old man, who was decorating their French Quarter cottage for Mardi Gras.

"What's this?" cried the old man. He began to chase the plastic baby, shouting, "Stop! Stop! You belong in the king cake!"

But the King Cake Baby ran on and teased:

"No, mon ami! You can't catch me, I'm the King Cake Baby!"

The old Creole woman and old Creole man tried, but they didn't get the baby.

The King Cake Baby sprinted through Jackson Square until he met a praline lady. "How you doing, dawlin'?" asked the praline lady. "You'd be perfect in my king cake! Come with me by my house."

"No way!" yelled the King Cake Baby. And off he dashed. The praline lady began to chase the plastic baby, shouting, "Stop! Stop! You belong in a king cake!" But the King Cake Baby ran on and teased:

The praline lady tried,
but she didn't get the baby.

Soon, the King Cake Baby met a waiter at Café du Monde. "Where y'at, Baby?" said the waiter. "Come on over here. Shouldn't you be in a king cake?"

"No way!" yelled the King Cake Baby. And off he dashed.

The waiter chased the plastic baby, shouting, "Stop! Stop! You belong in a king cake!"

But the King Cake Baby ran on and teased:

"No, mon ami! You can't catch me, I'm the King Cake Baby!"

The waiter tried, but he didn't get the baby.

The King Cake Baby was very proud that he could run so fast. "Nobody can catch me!" he thought.

As he neared the river, he met a baker. The King Cake Baby stopped to brag to the baker that he had run away from the old Creole woman, the old Creole man, the praline lady, and the waiter. "And I could run away from you, too!" he added.

"*C'est la vie,*" sighed the baker. "Run all you want. I am too old and slow and can't chase you." Then the baker asked, "Where you off to?"

The baby declared, "I'm going down the river on the *Creole Queen* riverboat."

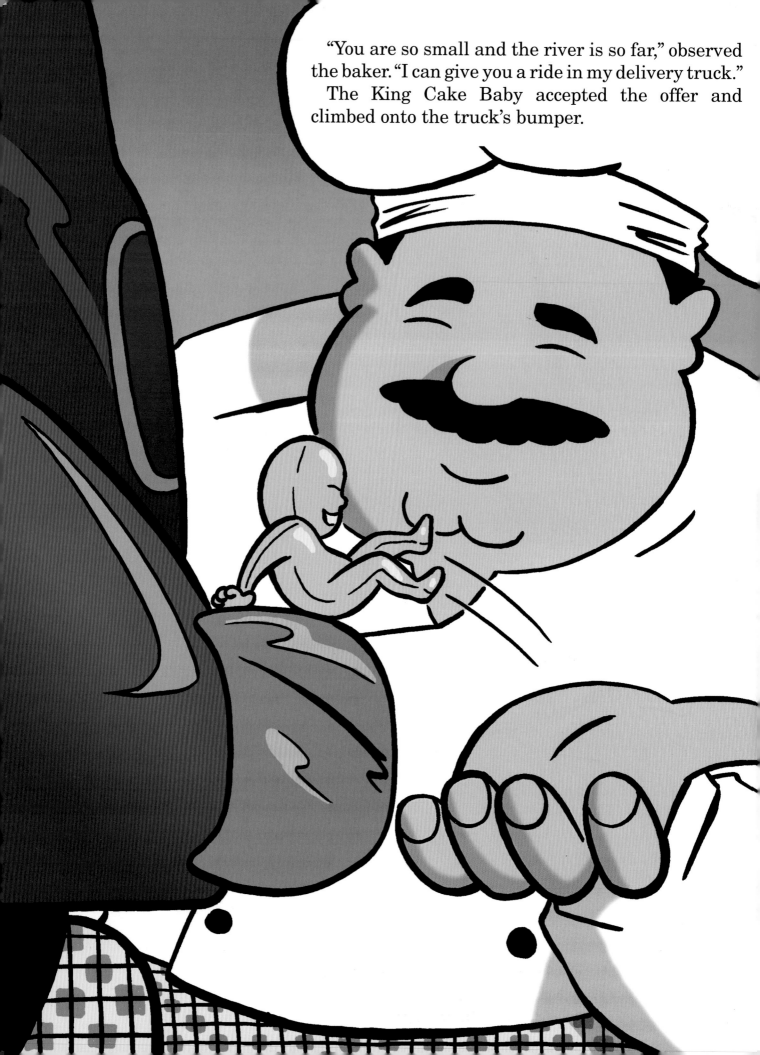

"You are so small and the river is so far," observed the baker. "I can give you a ride in my delivery truck."

The King Cake Baby accepted the offer and climbed onto the truck's bumper.

"Oh, Baby, I'm afraid you may fall off," the baker cautioned. "It's not safe on the bumper. Why don't you go inside the truck?"

M.BAKER

"Alright," agreed the baby. He moved inside and sat down in the back of the truck.

"Oh, Baby, I'm afraid there's no seatbelt back there," warned the baker. "It's not safe. Why don't you get inside of a cake box?"

"Yeah, you right," the baby said. But as he climbed inside, *swoosh!* The baker grabbed the plastic baby, stuffed him inside the king cake, and closed the lid.

"That's where a king cake baby belongs,"
thought the baker, "in a king cake."

Author's Note

The King Cake Baby is a humorous New Orleans tale based on the familiar plot and repetitive rhyme of the classic story of the Gingerbread Man. Like the King Cake Baby, the Gingerbread Man escapes from a kitchen and runs away from an old woman and an old man. A few new characters join the chase in this retelling, but in the end the King Cake Baby is snatched up, just as the Gingerbread Man is eventually caught and eaten by a sly fox. Try your hand at making your own king cake using the recipe below. *Bon appétit!*

Easy King Cake

Cake

2 loaves frozen white bread dough, thawed
½ cup granulated sugar
2 tablespoons cinnamon
4 tablespoons butter, melted
1 large, plastic king cake baby

1. Preheat the oven to 350 degrees.
2. In a bowl, mix together the sugar and cinnamon.
3. Roll the bread dough loaves into 9 x 11 rectangles and brush with melted butter.
4. Sprinkle one rectangle with half of the cinnamon-sugar mix. Sprinkle the remaining half on the second rectangle.
5. From one of the long sides, tightly roll each rectangle into a long tube.
6. Transfer the dough onto a cookie sheet, seam side down. Shape into an oval and connect the ends.
7. Bake until golden brown, approximately 30 minutes, or follow the baking directions on the bread dough package.
8. Don't forget to hide the king cake baby!

Toppings tip: Decorate your cake while it's still warm!

Cream-Cheese Icing

3 cups powdered sugar
4 ounces cream cheese, room temperature
3 tablespoons melted butter
¼ teaspoon vanilla extract
3 tablespoons milk

1. Mix all five ingredients in a bowl until the icing is thick enough to slowly drip from a whisk or spoon. Drizzle over the warm cake.

Colored Sugar

1½ cups white granulated sugar
3 drops red liquid food coloring
1 drop blue liquid food coloring
5 drops green liquid food coloring
5 drops yellow liquid food coloring
3 resealable plastic bags

1. Divide the sugar equally into three separate resealable bags.
2. Mix the red and blue food coloring together into the sugar in the first bag and knead gently to create the purple topping.
3. In the second bag, mix the sugar with the green food coloring.
4. Mix the yellow food coloring into the sugar in the third bag.
5. Sprinkle the purple, green, and gold sugar over the icing.